1001 THINGS

WE WOULD HAVE TOLD OUR KIDS

HAD THEY EVER LISTENED!!

by Judy Woods-Knight

Copyright © 1992 by Judy Woods-Knight. All rights reserved.

No part of this book may be reproduced without written permission from the publisher or copyright holder, except for a reviewer who may quote brief passages in a review; nor may any part of this book be reproduced, stored in a retrieval system, or transmitted in any form or by any means electronic, mechanical, photocopying, recording or other, without the written permission from the publisher or copyright holder.

This book is sold with the understanding that the subject matter covered herein is of a general nature and does not constitute legal, accounting or other professional advice for any specific individual or situation. Anyone planning to take action in any of the areas that this book describes should, of course, seek professional advice from accountants, lawyers, tax and other advisers, as would be prudent and advisable under their given circumstances.

R&E Publishers
P.O. Box 2008, Saratoga, CA 95070
Tel: (408) 866-6303   Fax: (408) 866-0825

Book Design and Typesetting by elletro Productions
Book Cover and Illustrations by Kaye Quinn

ISBN 0-88247-989-X

Designed, typeset and totally manufactured in the United States of America.

Lib. of Congress no. 92-50877

DEDICATION

I dedicate this book to those wise enough to make their families the center of their being and to my family who is more than worth that dedication.

Judy Woods-Knight

ACKNOWLEDGEMENT

To give proper credit to the various sources of inspiration for a book of this sort is difficult—although an effort has been made.

There is one thought that I have stolen outright, from a book entitled *Teacher As Actor*, by Morris Burns and Porter S. Woods. For caveat number five hundred forty-six, I wish to thank both Mr. Burns and Mr. Woods, my uncle.

FOREWARD

Several people who saw this manuscript before publication expressed the opinion that the information needed to be neatly separated and categorized. They were bothered by the fact that homely tips might be followed by profound thoughts or advice.

I resisted those suggestions since it is my feeling that family values are not transmitted neatly, but in a haphazard manner; "If you tell the truth, you don't have to remember what you said. Please take your hat off at the dinner table."

Does that sound familiar?

For better or worse, I thank the publisher, Bob Reed, for having agreed with me, or for having simply let me have my way.

Judy Woods-Knight

1. Read the classics.
2. Write a lot of letters.
3. Learn how to use a P.C.
4. Learn how to look things up.
5. Never make a joke at someone's expense.
6. Diet one week of each month.
7. Go to estate sales, garage sales, second-hand stores.
8. Never pay more than 1/3 of your monthly income on housing.
9. Learn how to wash windows with a squeegee.
10. It's easier to be on time than explain why you were late.

11. It's as easy to fill the top half of the gas tank as the bottom.

12. Own a calculator with a tape.

13. Save your old clothes, especially ties.

14. Nothing tastes as good as thin feels.

15. Read about other people's lives.

16. Turning the other cheek doesn't suggest masochism;
    it suggests looking at the other person's point of view.

17. ***MODERATION IN ALL THINGS INCLUDING MODERATION.***

18. Don't criticize something you don't understand
    from opera to mud wrestling.

19. Learn to speak another language fluently.

20. Know the difference between repression and positive thinking.

21. ***POSITIVE THINKING WORKS: POSITIVELY.***

22. Listen while you are being introduced instead of thinking of something clever to say next.

23. Go to films, by yourself.

24. Your younger siblings are **NOT** mom and dad's science project.

25. Always carry your family pictures with you during a move.

26. Volunteer your time.

27. Don't quote the Bible; live it.

28. Never throw gum on the sidewalk.

29. Don't buy anything packaged in plastic.

30. Listen to the rain on the roof.

31. If you are nice to your siblings, they will embarrass you less.

32. Keep track of old friends, high school and college buddies.

33. Always have an account to cover over-draft checks, automatically.

34. Always pay off credit cards each month.

35. Don't bounce a ball in the house.

36. Offer to baby sit for a retarded or handicapped child.

37. Offer to parent sit for a couple caring for their aged parents.

Judy Woods-Knight   *1001 THINGS...*

38.   Tell every mother that her baby is beautiful.

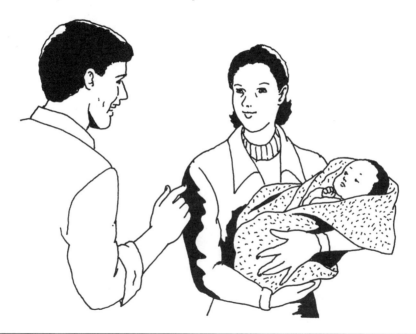

1001 THINGS...   *Judy Woods-Knight*

39. Grow your own herbs, tomatoes and vegetables.

40. Recycle everything.

41. **ALL SELFISHNESS IS SIN; ALL SIN IS SELFISHNESS.**

42. Stop eating when you're full.

43. Be honestly glad for other people.

44. Fidelity doesn't mean you're dead.

45. Trust your conscience.

46. Know that if you ignore it too often, your conscience retires.

47. Drink herbal tea.

48. Don't discount "home-remedies," or "Naturopathic medicine."

49. Always hang your clothes up, no matter how tired you are.

1001 THINGS...   *Judy Woods-Knight*

50.   Close the top of a potato chip sack with a couple of clothespins.

51.   Save rubber bands on an empty toilet paper roll.

52.   Care about minorities.

53.   When you are depressed,
            help someone more depressed than you.

54.   Always carry aspirin.

55.   Always have window cleaner in your car.

56.   Learn not to pop your "p's" while speaking in a microphone.

57.   Never take a good night's sleep for granted.

58.   Eat fresh vegetables and fruits in season.

59. Make your own jam.

60. Sing every chance you have.

61. Clean large plant leaves with used tea bags.

62. Never tell anyone proud of a dimple that it's just a hole in the muscle wall.

63. Say something supportive, once a day, to a family member or mate.

64. Refrain, once a day, from saying something unkind to same.

65. Know that if you praise your children, they usually don't believe you, but if you criticize them, they do.

66. ***KNOW THAT A YOUNGER SIBLING ALMOST ALWAYS TRUSTS YOU; RESIST ALL TEMPTATION TO WATCH THEM DESTROY THEMSELVES AND PUBLIC OR PRIVATE PROPERTY.***

67. Never tell anyone "this should be the best time of your life."

68. Never tell anyone they're lucky if they don't feel that way.

69. Never be "too cute."

70. Eat foreign foods.

71. Be the best cook you can be; experiment.

1001 THINGS...   *Judy Woods-Knight*

72. Be nice to salespersons; they don't expect it.

73. Clean your glasses several times a day.

74. Carry your toothbrush.

75. Be proud of America; we are a lovely, lively country.

76. Learn how to spell correctly; keep a list of difficult words.

77. Nothing is funnier than self-effacement, done correctly.

78. Speak to handicapped people.

79. Use the stairs rather than an elevator.

80. Never arrive early when invited to someone's house for a meal.

81. Always reciprocate when someone treats you to a meal; even if the person is older or you are single.

82. Always compliment a cook; even if it's your mother. (**ESPECIALLY** if it's your mother.)

83. Mark one calendar with important days like birthday's and anniversaries.

84. Never mix a sympathy card with one of congratulations.

85. Buy primroses for those you love after a long, hard winter.

86. Tell people when they make you happy.

87. Protect a "bimbo" every chance you have.

88. Put supportive notes in suitcases, lunch sacks, brief cases.

89. Be quick to admit you were a jerk; the quicker the better.

90. Watch Sesame Street all of your life.

91. Learn to meditate and practice yoga.

92. Meditation is not to imagine a perfect life but the tranquility to face the one you have.

93. Learn to put the em**PHAS**is on the right syl**LA**ble.

94. Always have clean fingernails, a clean handkerchief or tissues.

95. Remember the anniversary of a widowed person.

96. Never criticize your mate's mother or father.

97. Add a new word to your vocabulary a couple of times a week.

98. Resign from the Supreme Court; work on problems you can solve.

99. Write or call your parents once a week.

100. If your spouse is away, write or call every day.

101. Grow seasonal plants and flowers.

102. Don't talk about your trips
unless your listener shows sustained interest.

103. Always share your recipes.

104. Never assume anything.

105. Be continuously curious, inventive, creative.

106. Listen to classical music.

107. Blue houses don't sell.

108. Always leave time and date on a recorded message.

109. Carry an umbrella in your car.

110. Appreciate subtlety.

111. Take risks.

112. Be a cheerleader to yourself and those around you.

113. Appreciate and learn as much as you can about the human body.

114. ***IF YOU LOVE SOMEONE WHO LOVES YOU, REALIZE HOW LUCKY YOU ARE.***

115. Move when it's time to move;
don't renovate yourself out of the market.

116. Have compassion for everyone, including yourself.

117. Be sentimental; save graduation programs, old corsages, letters.

118. Ask old people about their lives.

119. Encourage a speaker with your attention, your nods and smiles; next time it could be you up there.

120. Never sit down on a public toilet seat, ill advisedly.

121. Train yourself to recognize humor, irony and pathos.

122. Take courses at local colleges; study things which interest you.

123. Do something you don't want to do everyday.

124. Always be planning, researching an interesting trip.

125. Go camping at least once.

126. Bake your own bread; begin with frozen, unraised loaves.

127. Leave your mind open to reincarnation;
a concept two thirds of the world believes.

128. **CONSIDER** reincarnation as a possible explanation
for homosexuality.

129. Be unhappy for those who suffer, regardless of the reason.

130. Neurosis is born when a child finds his/her home is not a safe haven
and his/her parents unreliable, or just not very nice.

131. *DON'T HAVE CHILDREN TO ENHANCE YOUR LIFE,
BUT TO GIVE THEM ONE.*

132. One parent needs to stay home with a young children for **AS LONG AS POSSIBLE.**

133. In the single paycheck, single parent family, the child often has neither a father nor a mother.

134. Imagine the world if each family truly nurtured and tried to meet the needs of each member all of the time. Make the thought your reality.

135. Being at home with children can be boring, repetitive and dull.

136. Working can be boring, repetitive and dull.

137. It's definitely OK to deny yourself something you really want.

138. Buy a recording of The Bible, read by a professional.

139. Never discuss how religious you are.

140. Know that whatever your problem, there's an answer.

141. God answers all of our prayers. Sometimes He says no.

142. Universal truths are not universal; culture dictates right and wrong.

143. Never place the roll-on deodorant next to the roll-on shoe polish.

144. When calling a long list of people, make certain you remember where you are on that list.

145. If you dial a wrong number, apologize before you hang up.

146. Always get the name of someone helping you on the telephone.

147. What goes around comes around.

148. A child should earn his/her allowance.

149. Be able to identify a hundred trees by name and species.

150. Learn the rules to every game you play.

151. Take a walk every day.

152. Don't confuse sitcoms and morality.

153. Watch lots of old black and white movies.

154. Practice restraint, gentleness.

155. On an airplane, take slipper socks in your carry on luggage.

156. When packing for a trip, select what you need then take half.

157. While travelling always drink bottled water, even in the USA.

158. Leaving your Christmas lights up all year long is tacky.

159. Plastic flowers and flamingos are even worse.

160. Never talk with food in your mouth.

161. Always be reading at least two good books.

162. Coupons can drive you crazy.

163. Experiment with oil or acrylic painting.

164. Some time during your life, take an art history class.

165. Necessity is the mother of a good thing like invention and a bad thing like crime.

166. There is a big difference between questioning and criticizing; one is an information gathering exercise and the other is a dead end.

167. A person tempted away from one marriage is likely to repeat the performance.

168. Be kind to your teachers; they have a very hard job.

169. At a party or a conference, make it a point to talk with someone who looks more uncomfortable than you might feel.

170. Never leave a party without thanking the host or hostess.

171. Never drink or serve anything stronger than beer or wine.

172. Never throw your knowledge around.

173. Never assume that entertaining is easy for anyone.

174. Never confuse "Pam" with "Easy Off."

175. There is no excuse for being rude.

176. Own a down quilt.

177. Always buy comfortable shoes, regardless of the cost.

178. Own more than one pair of glasses.

179. You cannot give yourself away; it's impossible.

180. It's easier to floss than to apologize to your hygienist.

181. No one on their death bed ever said,
"I wish I had been less devoted to my family."

182. ***IF YOU ARE A VICTIM: LOOK TO YOUR PERPETRATOR FOR RESTITUTION OR CONCILIATION, NOT ANSWERS.***

183. Perpetrators don't have answers; they have urges.

184. ***YOU KNOW YOU ARE IN LOVE WHEN THE PERSON YOU LOVE MAKES YOU LOVE YOURSELF BETTER.***

185. No one can define love; they can only describe how it feels.

186. Love should make you feel good;
if it doesn't it's not love but something else.

187. Lots of things that feel good are bad for you.

188. Lots of things that feel bad are good for you.

189. You can be in control of what you think.

190. Make it positive.

191. Resentment can eat you alive.

192. ***IF YOU CANNOT CHANGE A BAD SITUATION CHANGE YOUR REACTION TO IT.***

193. Heart attacks happen to people who have an unrealistic sense of time urgency coupled with massive doses of hostility.

194. Many adults who commit suicide honestly think they are doing their families a favor.

195. Depression is about seeing no way out.

196. Never presume that someone has fewer problems than you.

197. Suicide ranks third in all teenage deaths.

198. Research from the University of Washington and the University of Tennessee revealed that fact. In addition, they found that having a gun in the house increases the likelihood of suicide five-fold.

199. *OWNING A GUN IS ALWAYS DANGEROUS.*

200. When our forefathers wrote the Bill of Rights, a rifle weighed twenty pounds and was accurate up to fifty feet.

201. Have the courage to support the simple solution.

202. There are many times in a good marriage when love disappears, all together.

203. There are many times when love returns fuller than ever before.

204. *BE STILL AND KNOW.*

205. People get married when they have to.

206. Everyone wants to marry "a bargain," the unattainable.

207. When you get married your bed includes a lot of people; both sets of parents not to mention step parents, former loves....

208. Offspring from happy marriages often make bad ones, assuming that marriage is easy.

209. Unlike abused children, children from dysfunctional marriages do not often repeat their parent's mistakes. They make different ones.

210. Women are usually the "keeper of the keys" as far as premarital sex is concerned. It's not that this is right or good; it just is.

211. A woman who permits premarital sex is taking a real chance with the relationship.

212. A woman who does not indulge in premarital sex is taking a real chance with the relationship.

213. It takes more than practice to make sex meaningful.

214. A lot of men give love to get sex.

215. A lot of women give sex to get love.

216. A lot of people give sex for no reason at all.

217. Sex was not designed to be recreational.

218. Sex was designed to be an enigma.

219. Sex is just one physical expression of love.

220. It is difficult, if not impossible, to discuss sex intelligently with your partner.

221. Bette Davis called sex "God's biggest joke."

222. There is nothing funny about sex.

223. ***WE DON'T THINK TOO MUCH ABOUT SEX, WE THINK TOO LITTLE OF IT.***

224. Even "old" couples can have "lose yourself sex."

225. There is no substitute for cleanliness or trust in a sexual relationship.

226. Repeating your marriage vows is a positive experience.

227. Learn how to argue effectively.

228. Contrary to popular belief, if a marriage is in trouble, often a bigger, shared problem helps. Building a house, having a baby, moving to a new location all relieve the focus of tension.

229. Husbands often feel jealous over the attention a new baby gets.

230. Women often feel resentful over the amount of attention a new baby requires.

231. A woman needs to be reminded that she's still sexy after she's had a baby.

232. A new mother needs to be reminded, often, that she will someday get her life back.

233. A new father needs to be reminded, even more often, that someday he will have his wife back.

234. A new father needs to give his wife a "free nap" frequently.

235. Babies are universally cross at dinner time.

236. A real man shares in the household and child care chores without being asked or expecting praise.
He should be lavished with praise, anyway.

1001 THINGS...   *Judy Woods-Knight*

237. Comfort your babies,
hold them,
make them feel secure
and loved.
They are so little
and feel uncomfortable
a lot of the time.

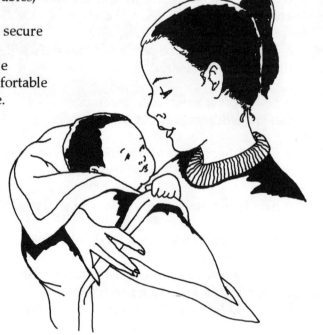

238. If someone is trying to help you with your new baby, don't expect them to do things "your way."

239. Don't worry about spoiling a baby.

240. ***PARENTHOOD IS NOT A CONTEST OF WILLS.***

241. Stimulate your baby with bright colors, your voice, singing, music and body contact.

242. When they cannot be comforted, try turning on stirring music, the vacuum cleaner or take them, regardless of the hour, for a ride in the car.

243. Look at your child when you feed them. Help them connect your face, your voice with the good feeling of being nourished.

244. Never forget how you felt when your baby was sick. Save that memory for a time when they're in their teens.

245. Keep the corniest baby book you care to; this is your right.

246. Add to that book for the rest of your life if you feel like it.

247. Thank God, every day, for a normal child.

248. Thank God, every day, for a handicapped child;
you can learn so much from them.

249. If you cannot have children, love someone else's child.
There are plenty of children who need love. Find them.

250. Teach your children to recognize a paragraph;
a difficult concept for most children to learn.

251. Take turns reading from a storybook each night with your child.

252. Bake chocolate chip cookies on rainy days.

253. Raw cookie dough is very good for you.

254. Throw some food coloring and soap suds into your child's bath to make it an adventure.

255. Watch good children's films together.

256. Instigate family rituals surrounding all of the holidays; life can't have too many little celebrations.

257. Read Dickens' A Christmas Carol aloud every Christmas season.

258. Tell your children about God.

259. Tell them as much as they want to know about where babies come from. Trust your instincts; get a model or a diagram of the human body and do a lot of pointing.

260. Tell them funny stories about when you were a kid.

261. Create excitement
in your children's lives;
long walks, picnics,
trips to parks, zoos.
Take them to the library,
a museum, swimming, in a boat,
a ferry, to a fish hatchery, a farm.
Take them to a train station,
an airport, a fire station.

262. Record the your children's voices as they grow.

263. Ask your children about their problems,
     but don't take it personally, if they don't want to talk.

264. Have a few reasonable chores which you allow them to perform on their own schedule, whenever possible.

265. Sometimes a spanking can clear the air. (What kind of permanent damage can you do to a psyche that is asking for a light swat and a butt that is covered with thick diapers and a pair of Levi's?)

266. Tell your siblings and your kids you love them; unconditionally.

267. No one really loves anyone unconditionally,
     but make the effort.

268. Don't freak-out if kids are picky eaters. Give them vitamins, milk and endure. They'll do better if you're cheerful.

1001 THINGS...   *Judy Woods-Knight*

269. Show your kids that you love their Dad/Mother, their Grandparents.

270. Give lots of hugs and kisses, as long as they will let you.

271. Respect their wishes when they don't want hugs and kisses.
(Remember when I used to pay you guys a dollar for a kiss? Thatwas the wrong message to send about love and money...)

272. Don't become discouraged if you mess up a situation.
Kids are very forgiving.

273. Every child wants to love and live with his/her own parents.

274. Every child wants to be proud of his/her own parents.

275. Take an active interest in their school work,
but don't be too quick to take sides when there is a problem. Meet with the teacher.

276. It is your less than elevating duty to help your children with their weekly spelling words and their multiplication tables.

277. Encourage (bribe?) your children to read a book a week; two in the summer.

278. Every child should learn how to do his/her own laundry.

279. Every child should learn how to sew on a button.

280. Every child should learn how to cook and clean up the mess.

281. Every child should work and be responsible for buying his/her own clothes or earning his/her own spending money and car insurance.

282. Every child should learn to baby sit.

283. If a child has to baby sit his siblings, he should be given advance notice and paid something.

284. Every child
should see the ocean,
climb a mountain,
fish in a stream,
go to a fair,
join a club,
play a sport,
go to Sunday school.

285. Always remember how badly you wanted to "fit in."

286. Don't be rigid about dress codes.

287. Remember that a child was born with his personality; the good stuff like being funny and the bad stuff like putting things off.

288. Nobody, even you, was as perfect a child as you remember.

289. Nobody, even you, was as bad as you remember.

290. Your mother and sometimes your father will always forgive you, regardless of what you've done. (To the end, Ted Bundy's mother referred to her son as "my darling boy.")

291. ***NOBODY'S DOING THE BEST THEY CAN.***

292. We are all merely trying to cope, operating with limited vision and our own self-interest.

1001 THINGS...   *Judy Woods-Knight*

293. It's a lot easier to hate a person, place or thing than to love a person, place or thing.

294. Being positive, enthusiastic, cheerful, generous, vulnerable and forgiving is to leave yourself wide open for a slam dunk.

295. That's OK if you learn the artful dodge.

296. The person who likes himself has done his homework.

297. We are much harder on ourselves than we are on anyone else.

298. It is human nature to forget the many positive things people say about us.

299. It is also human nature to internalize all the negatives.

300. "Human nature, Mr. Allnut, was what we were put in this world to rise above." (From The African Queen)

301. Learn about religions other than your own.

302. Arguing about religion is to lose the point.

303. If God is perfect, why did He create us?

304. It boggles the mind to think of infinity; who wants to even enjoy themselves forever?

305. A perfect example of prayer is Tevyer from Fiddler on the Roof.

306. Eventually things "even up." That's why bad things happen to good people and why good things happen to bad people.

307. Hell is probably served right here on earth.

308. Everyone should read about "near death" experiences.

309. Attending a church or synagogue is not a chore, it's elevating.

310. The best way to encourage anyone to go to church is to demonstrate that attending makes you better, happier, more tolerant, forgiving.

311. Many Christians consider the ten commandments the "Ten Suggestions."

312. Listen to the Messiah at least once a year.

313. Learn everything you can about Indian lore.

314. Everything in nature is cyclic.

315. Everything in nature is complex.

316. Everything in nature is connected to everything else.

317. If nothing in nature happens in a haphazard manner, how can anyone presume the creation of the world was an accident?

318. You don't have to believe in Adam and Eve. You don't have to believe in the Great Flood or believe in any kind of literal interpretation of The Bible, only that it was inspired by God to help us live a good life.

319. We need to believe that the universe was created by The Creator.

320. To have a baby, to paint a picture, write a story, a symphony or a song, is to share in that creation.

321. It would be a very grave mistake to consider one's God given talents as anything but.

322. We will all be judged on what we did with our talents. They were given us to use, explore and share.

323. Many people spend their energies exploring areas outside their natural talents, often squandering and losing them.

324. On-going self-exploration is scary but necessary.

325. It is a shock to look in the mirror or at your reflection in a store window as you get older.

326. Nobody totally likes the way they look.

327. Some people like the way they look for short periods of time; say forty-five minutes to an hour.

328. It makes most of us uncomfortable to hear our recorded voice.

329. Most people have no idea how others see them.
That's probably a blessing.

330. Everyone has embarrassing moments.

331. The more pompous, patronizing and pragmatic you are, the more hilarious (to others) are your embarrassing experiences.

332. There is no way to avoid embarrassing moments other than to consistently think in terms of cause and effect.

333. Dwelling on "what if's" can make a person safer but deadly dull.

334. Having too many gadgets guarding against theft advertises that you've got a lot of good stuff.

335. Some people have so many safety devises, computerized locks, signs, decals, whistles and bells that it's normal to fanaticize about robbing them.

336. With the possible exception of a Stradivarius violin, your family heirlooms and photos, **ANYTHING CAN BE REPLACED**.

337. Don't purchase anything you couldn't bear to lose.

338. Some people can't see the forest for the trees, while others have trouble just finding the forest.

339. The only really important things in life are relationships, accomplishments, memories and dreams. These are worth guarding and protecting with your last breath.

340. The richest people are often the stingiest.

341. The most generous people are often the poorest.

342. There is a thin line between good ecology and pure nuttiness.

343. Saving lint from one's dryer trap for stuffing pillows is nutty; saving it to light fireplaces fires is smart.

344. Madonna has gone beyond sexual to become asexual.

345. Americans are obsessed with their own body odors.

346. Everyone should recycle everything they can.

347. Don't litter; help clean-up.

348. There is no substitute for your own teeth.

349. Always take a bath before a doctor's appointment.

350. You are only a temporary visitor in your body; be generous with it by donating blood and becoming an organ donor.

351. Read articles about newlyweds, those celebrating their fiftieth anniversaries and obituaries for insight into real human drama.

352. Be selective about TV viewing.

353. Know that the child watching too many family sitcoms may be sending a message.

354. Own a good, sharp pair of scissors.

1001 THINGS...   *Judy Woods-Knight*

355. Own a good, expensive knife set.

356. Take a first aid course and practice CPR.

357. Always have "syrup of ipecac" on hand to induce vomiting.

358. Have a lot of boring things like a working flashlight, candles, matches, fire-extinguisher, hot pads, cold packs, bandages, elastic wraps, rubbing alcohol, thermometer, aspirin, antacids, Benadryl (for allergic reactions) Bacitracin (an antiseptic ointment) and a vaporizer in your home.

359. Nothing feels as good to a person suffering from a chest cold as Vick's VapoRub and a towel you've (carefully) warmed in the oven.

360. Nothing feels better to someone with poison oak or chicken pox than to put a cup or two of uncooked oatmeal in an old nylon in their tub of lukewarm water.

361. There is no substitute for chicken soup regardless of your ethnicity.

362. Everyone should have a medical encyclopedia.

363. Not everyone can read it without developing a lot of serious-sounding symptoms.

364. Don't let doctors scare you. You know a lot more about your body or your child's than they do. If they make you uncomfortable, tell them so or find a new doctor.

365. If going to the dentist is a trauma, ask about nitrous oxide. (Laughing Gas)

366. Apprehension is worse than pain.

367. Anxiety is worse than anything.

368. *THERE IS NO SUCH THING AS REALITY.*

369. There is only one's perception concerning what is real.

370. The tooth fairy is a nice concept. We don't encourage our kids to believe enough in fairies for reasons too sad to discuss.

371. Why build up the Santa Claus myth when the Christmas Story is a beautiful choice?

372. Children are born inherently unkind and brutally frank.

373. Children can be, must be, sensitized as soon as possible. (Use personal stories, anecdotes, rewards, vague threats, books, videos. This is life's first and most important, on-going lesson.)

374. Self-esteem is never gained at another's expense.

375. It never has been a matter of whether a man is smarter than a woman; it isn't whether a man is stronger, more capable, flexible, reliable, creative. What has held some women back is the

fact that they are more cyclic. (Meaning that sometimes we are even better than before.)

376. Morning sickness might be the body's reaction to the environment or foods the fetus cannot yet tolerate.

377. Bad habits and bad behavior are highly contagious.

378. Good habits or behavior are rarely "catching."

379. ***ONLY YOU CAN LET SOMEONE HURT YOU.***

380. No matter how supportive and understanding your parents may be, there are platoons of other people ready to make your childhood a pretty terrible time.

381. ***EVERYONE HAD A PAINFUL CHILDHOOD. THAT'S WHY IT WAS PUT FIRST; TO GET IT OUT OF THE WAY.***

382. You will always have, inside you, the small child you once were.

383. It's one of life's missions to understand that child.

384. To taunt, tease, humiliate or break the spirit of another person is to kill a little part of them.

385. Only insecure people try to gain security from creating misery in others.

386. To watch child abuse and to ignore it is to be an accomplice.

387. To remain in a marriage in which your spouse abuses you or your children is a criminal act of cowardice.

388. Everyone needs to develop a marketable skill.

389. Volunteering your time, taking night courses, perfecting your talents or skills at home; all enhance your employment opportunities.

390. No job is more demeaning than a lifetime of abuse or of public assistance.

391. Everyone deserves a nurtured childhood. After that, no one owes you anything.

392. The status quo is always easier.

393. Status quo never improved anyone's life.

394. Never lose sight of the fact that virtually everyone is scared.

395. What separates people is those who work through these scary feelings and those who cave into them.

396. Most people cannot tell when another is petrified; they are too self-absorbed.

1001 THINGS... *Judy Woods-Knight*

397. The few who are sensitive enough to notice that you are afraid will also be sensitive enough to help you.

398. The best success was never the "easy win."

399. Keep everyone informed; bad news doesn't get better with time.

400. ***SCRATCH WHERE IT ITCHES;
NOT WHERE IT LOOKS THE BEST.***

401. Be nice to the people you meet on the way up; you may meet them again on the way down.

402. Be nice to everyone regardless of your current direction.

403. Change your sheets once a week; your underwear daily.

404. Eat at the table; TV in the "off" position.

405. Have friends to dinner, often. Set the nicest table you can.

406. If you can read, you can cook...eventually.

407. If you have to move in with your parents after you are married, don't.

408. Use your blender to make your own salad dressing.

409. Don't be afraid to be controversial.

410. Practical people have the annoying habit of squelching the fires of the original thinkers.

411. We need original thinkers.

412. We need practical thinkers.

413. We need tolerance.

414. There is no such thing as a "bad" word; only bad actions.

415. No child was ever born bad; it happens hit by hit.

416. A promise is a sacred thing.

417. Never go back on a promise even if you get a better deal.

418. Innocence cannot be replaced, but it can be rekindled; reborn.

419. Credibility, once lost is hard to regain.

420. Never rely on charm. To do so is a form of prostitution.

421. It is possible to be charming, productive and dependable.

422. Never hold a grudge more than twenty-four hours.

423. Always go home with the person who brought you.

424. A man should always think he initiated the relationship.

425. ***WHAT IS TRUE IS NOT ALWAYS RIGHT.***

426. If the chemistry isn't there, forget it.

427. Obsessive people aren't always crazy,
but they can drive normal people certifiably insane.

428. You will never forget your first love, even if it was a lousy experience.

429. There is something classically beautiful in unrequited love.

430. No one really knows another person until they're married. And then you both change.

431. That's what makes marriage interesting; the constant change.

432. You will be rewarded for staying true to your marriage vows.

433. If you slip, never tell anyone except a trusted counselor.

434. Of all the emotions guilt is the hardest to bear.

435. Without guilt, forty-five thousand psychiatrists would be on food stamps.

436. Know that changing mates means changing troubles.

437. Learn to talk and walk together.

438. Work at being your mate's best friend; work at making him/her yours.

439. Select thoughtful gifts for each other.

440. Read or reread *The Gift of the Magi* by O. Henry.

441. Jealousy has very little to do with love
and a lot to do with ownership.

442. Rape has nothing to do with sex
and everything to do with power.

443. Suicide is a permanent solution to a temporary problem.

444. Kids join gangs because they need identity,
want to "belong."
Families, churches, and youth groups
were designed to fill that need.

445. Riots are about pent-up frustration,
helplessness, isolation,
a lack of self-worth,
guidance and direction;
not government money.

1001 THINGS...   *Judy Woods-Knight*

446. Elementary schools were designed to teach reading, mathematics, writing and correct spelling. They were also designed to teach geography, social studies, proper English, writing skills, music, art and physical education.

447. Today, schools are expected to do all of this plus feed many students breakfast and lunch. They are frequently expected to treat minor emergencies and care for sick children whose parents cannot be reached. They must insure that students are inoculated, free of head lice, test their vision, their hearing, examine their teeth, their spines.

448. Schools are expected to teach self-esteem, sex education, personal safety, "home-alone skills," fire safety, bike safety, how to behave around strange animals, self-defense against sex-offenders and kidnappers.

449. Schools attempt to teach coping skills, stress and anger management, racial harmony, racial pride, English as a second language and personal hygiene.

450. Schools are expected to report abusive treatment, evaluate learning disorders, abnormal attention spans and provide a large range of remedial courses as well as accelerated study for gifted students.

451. Schools are expected to absorb handicapped children, transient children and children with aggressive, disturbing personalities.

452. Teachers are expected to keep parents informed about their child's progress academically, socially, physically and emotionally. They are expected to be good role models for their students, treating each child as an individual, with patience and fairness.

453. A teacher is expected to go to extraordinary means to reach a parent of a student about whom she might be concerned. A teacher is expected to have an attractive, stimulating classroom and to provide field trips and other diversions to promote and enrich the learning of her students often using her own money. At the drop of a hat, she is

expected to write detailed at-home work for students who are ill, absorb a new student or listen to the concerns expressed by parents. She is expected to enthusiastically support any school sponsored event and take on special assignments such as assemblies, plays or musical events.

454. A teacher is expected to have detailed lesson plans done well in advance and to continue her education during her off-duty hours or summers.

455. It is currently suggested that our schools undertake the responsibility for teaching moral values.

456. To do all of this effectively; **BE PREPARED TO SPEND THE MONEY AND TO ADD TO THE CURRENT CALENDER YEAR.**

457. *THE PUBLIC SCHOOL SHOULD NOT BE EXPECTED TO DO THE JOB OF GOOD AND CARING PARENTS.*

458. If you can keep your head when those around you lose theirs, it may be that you don't totally understand the situation.

459. Give me a student with an average IQ and a good attitude.

460. Teaching would be a joy if every child were sent to school untroubled and ready to learn.

461. The student's mistrust of adults is a major detraction to learning.

462. Disillusionment with adults can currently be detected in pre-school.

463. ***THERE IS NO WORSE CRIME THAN TO BETRAY THE TRUST OF THOSE IN YOUR CARE.***

464. The quickest way to undermine a culture is through its children.

465. Governments should be judged on how they treat the least among them.

466. Every man was not created equal. That's why some men deserve even more compassion than others.

467. Morality cannot be legislated but fairness can. (Martin Luther King)

468. ***EVERYONE IN THEIR HEART OF HEARTS BELIEVES THEMSELVES UNIQUE.***

469. Every man is unique.

470. To know that you are unique is not to place yourself above the law but to make you responsible *for* the law.

471. Prejudice is about lumping people together as a group.

472. "There are two tragedies in life. One is to lose your heart's desire. The other is to gain it." (George Bernard Shaw)

473. "**JUST BE YOURSELF**," is not always good advice.

474. Self-centeredness is now socially acceptable and wrong.

475. How terrible to devote all of your energies to your education, your training, your career. To concentrate on your own interests, your body, wardrobe, hobbies and sports. How awful to pursue your own hopes, aspirations and dreams to find that what they want at the top is a family person with selfless, altruistic vision.

476. If you want to be at the top; know that is where the tough questions land. The easier ones are handled somewhere else.

477. Oprah Winfrey is doing good.

478. If it's so healthy to cry, why does it cause a headache?

479. Arrogance is patently unforgivable.

480. Elvis Presley died from dumbness.

481. Marilyn Monroe died from vulnerability.

482. JFK died from charisma.

483. Robert Kennedy died from complicity.

484. We do not haunt these restless souls; they haunt us.

485. ***LIVE TO REST IN PEACE.***

486. It's important to be loved for the right reasons.

487. No one has a good time at a wedding.

488. The secret to a happy marriage is **THE DIVISION OF LABOR**.

489. Among other things, the division of labor defines who takes out the garbage, when, where and how often.

490. To empty the garbage is human, to put in a new liner is divine.

491. There are many important things done best in the rain; working, writing, reading, thinking, making love, to name but a few....

492. Never give up your dream, but meanwhile keep your day job.

493. Never do business with someone who stars in their own commercials. (With the possible exception of Uncle Sam.)

494. Never buy anything from someone who points at you, with the certain exception of Uncle Sam.

495. Never bank with someone operating from a trailer.

496. The two happiest days of our lives were the day we bought our trailer and the day we sold it.

497. Don't visit someone in the hospital for a short stay. Send them something and visit them when they're feeling better.

498. Our culture takes drugs except when they really need them.

499. Joan Rivers once described childbirth as a "scream." Lamaz describes childbirth as something which can be totally painless and physically gratifying. Who's right? (Answer rhymes with "quivers.")

500. To laugh elevates a person beyond the condition of his despair.

501. Forget how much you resent the French when you visit Paris, the most beautiful city in the world.

502. If you find the Louvre overpowering, visit the Impressionist's galleries in the Tuileries Gardens, the Jue de Paumne and the Orangerie.

503. You were given your family for a reason.

504. You don't have to love them, but to protect, understand, visit, encourage, help and forgive your family all the days of your life.

505. We knew one perfectly happy couple but he died.

506. Everyone, even a woman, needs a wife.

507. Bring in a shopping cart someone else left in the parking lot.

508. Know that violent and explicit TV hurts children.

509. Get a pet and pray that it likes your children better than it likes you.

510. *ALWAYS SMILE AT LITTLE KIDS.*

511. Consider any child lost in a store to be your responsibility.

512. Go to church bazaars and buy something you like and something carefully done but pathetic.

513. Ask to see your friend's wedding pictures.

514. No one should be exposed to graphic advertisements concerning bodily functions because....

515. If an advertisement offends you, write the company.

516. High fashion is capricious, expensive and silly.

517. Always buy gas at the station where you get a free car wash.

518. Never ask a professional a professional question at a party; ask for an appointment.

519. Free advice is usually over-priced.

520. Accept the fact that you are someone's role model with patience and grace.

521. Accept the fact that you are the butt of someone's joke with the same patience and the same grace.

522. Thank someone who insults you. To do this stops them and may, incidently, draw others to your defense.

523. Never give a present you don't want for yourself.

524. Greeting cards are too expensive. Order calling cards to include with gifts and on other special occasions, write a note.

525. "Recycle" the clever cards you receive.

526. Learn to read a map.

527. Never be the first man on the wrong road.

528. Learn to change a tire; your own.

529. Learn to read music.

530. Own a keyboard as soon as you can.

531. Never kill a mosquito with a hatchet or beat a dead horse.

532. Cut your losses.

533. You should never "should" on anyone.

534. Never give or attend a party with the idea of selling something.

535. ***NEVER PUT SOMEONE ON THE SPOT AND CALL IT ASSERTIVENESS.***

536. Make certain your mate thinks you put them above your work.

537. It's not only OK to go to bed angry, it's probably the only way anyone's going to get any sleep.

538. In the morning, solve the problem, which now probably looks a lot clearer.

539. A compromise is something you do that neither one likes at all.

540. Develop a short-hand between you and your spouse for special occasions; when you feel romantic, when you want to cut an argument short, when you want to make an instant apology, when you think they're boring the company. (How about them Phillies?)

541. Never admit that you hated the book someone recommended when you can honestly admit "that was some book!"

542. Learn to say "no," effectively. What part of that word could be confusing?

543. You do not owe anyone a long explanation or apology after you've declined something you do not wish to do.

544. You should learn to "throw" your voice; to speak from the diaphragm.

545. Learn all you can about body language.

546. In language and in algebra, two positives make a positive and two negatives still make a positive. (Sure, sure!)

547. Familiarize yourself with your rented car before you roar off into the darkness.

548. Never call your wife "the little woman."

549. ***TWO WRONGS DON'T MAKE A RIGHT.***

550. ***TWO RIGHTS CAN MAKE A WRONG.***

551. Marriage is not a 50/50 proposition; it's closer to 100% on each side, 50% of the time.

552. Never give a kitten as a door-prize.

553. Never tell anyone something they've said was "the dumbest thing I've ever heard."

554. Always keep your repair manuals in one place;
together, forever.

555. Play the music from your courting days.

556. Learn to square dance, clog, polka. Learn to do an Irish jig and the Highland Fling.

557. Unless you are paralyzed from the waist down, there is no excuse for not dancing with a wife who has had her hair done, bought a new dress and is excited about the evening.

558. To dance, you hold a person close, relax and move in time with the music. It's a lot easier than golf.

559. *RESPECT PEOPLE WHO KNOW HOW TO FIX THINGS.*

560. Never confuse reticence with selfishness.

561. Sunday night is the time most people come down with head colds.

562. **TIP STRAIGHT FROM HELOISE:** During a party, put packaged ice in the drum of your washing machine to keep canned beverages cold. When the party's over, remove the remaining cans, drain the melted water.

563. **A COCKTAIL PARTY**: Where people are upset about smoking. A place where no one sits down or has a meaningful conversation. A place where you're never close to someone you'd like to talk to, something you'd like to eat, or the napkins. A time when you cannot easily eat and drink at the same time, cannot talk and eat at the same time. A time when you worry about spilling, spotting, spitting and splitting.

564. Deep breathing meditation is as easy as 1-2-3.

565. You should meditate twenty minutes every day.

566. Remember the feeling you have in your chest when you're happy. You can approximate the good feeling with deep breathing.

567. When held-up in a long, slow line, look at other people and wish for something you think they might need.

568. Consider each new misery a benchmark.

569. Bring your old magazines along to leave in waiting rooms or other places you think they might be appreciated.

570. If possible, marry someone uglier than you.

571. Marry someone smart in different ways than you.

572. *OPPOSITES ATTRACT, THEN WE ATTEMPT TO MAKE THEM MORE LIKE US.*

573. In an argument, the following words should be avoided: clearly, naturally, rightfully, innocently, obviously, certainly, absolutely, unquestionably, henceforth....

574. Always get it in writing.

575. "A verbal contract isn't worth the paper it's printed on." (Samuel Goldwyn, attributed)

576. When treated to dinner, offer to pay for the drinks or the tip.

577. When treated to dinner, order from the medium price-range.

578. Always have emergency money or a spare check tucked away.

579. Is our government
    a) a triumph of bad management over poor planning?
    b) a triumph of poor planning over bad management?

580. To facilitate filing your taxes;
     a) list all earnings, dividends revenues in column A
     b) add column A
     c) send a check written in that amount to the IRS.

581. If you have a toothache, use oil of cloves on a cotton swab.

582. If you have a cough; sleep sitting up and suck on a lemon.

583. Remember JFK for his easy grace answering tough questions.

584. Nobody is all good or all bad.

585. Always give someone whose birthday falls in December a thoughtfully chosen present wrapped in birthday paper.

586. A good marriage is strengthened by lots of little things like the cheerful use of earplugs.

587. Never tell anyone that they are tone deaf.

588. The human body has locked within itself the power to cure its ills.

589. That's why being in touch with your body is so important.

590. ***YOUR FRAME OF MIND HAS EVERYTHING TO DO WITH YOUR IMMUNE SYSTEM.***

591. The best way to learn to use a computer is one-on-one.

592. No one knew the true meaning of calamity until the invention of the computer.

593. If plumbers charge such exorbitant rates, why do they still carry lunchpails and live in modest neighborhoods?

594. A good wedding present is a rice steamer or a photograph album with little plastic envelopes holding your most successful recipes.

595. Our funerals are macabre and expensive; just like our weddings.

596. American's don't know how to properly "mark the day."

597. The world is divided between those who put off until next Thursday that which should be done today and those who would do today that which would better be done next Thursday.

598. Look for the motive behind the motive.

599. It's definitely OK if everyone doesn't like you, but you should strive to like everyone you meet.

600. ***I WOULDN'T BE PARANOID IF EVERYBODY DIDN'T HATE ME.***

601. When you feel blue, write something cheerful to someone you think feels worse.

602. Learn to make good soup; soup makes something good out of life's little left overs. It is unpretentious, non-fatting, inexpensive yet filling. Soup never asks you to eat it before you're ready, but sits on the back burner, making your kitchen smell full of promise. Soup advertises neither affluence or poverty, only a careful cook. You can offer soup to a sick child or a visiting king. It can be humble, honest, soothing or provocative, teasing and full of spice.
Soup is the poetry of life.

603. Left overs: another chance to excel.

604. Never eat before you give a speech, if you can avoid it.

605. Never drink milk before you sing.

606. Heat syrup and add a shot of bourbon before you use it.

607. Always support local theater, art or symphony group.

608. If you know a struggling artist, buy some of his/her work.

609. Know your blood type.

610. Don't criticize a scientist, statistician or accountant for being less than sensitive.

611. Never criticize an artist, writer or poet for being vague or disorganized.

612. One of the aims of higher education is to supply the left-brained student right-brained skills and vice-versa. That's why college is so hard.

613. If you're broke, you can make a good meal from oriental noodles.

614. Almost no one remembers how clean your house was but how glad you were to see them and what you gave them to eat and drink.

615. Your children will remember you for how kind, how patient you were, how you listened and what you gave them. Graveyards are full of women who tried to do too much more than that.

616. Dr. Spock saved a whole generation a lot of grief.

617. Parents need to continuously study parenting the same way they would any other major undertaking.

618. Bangkok is a remarkably beautiful Asian city.

619. Malaysia is one place we know where antiques are plentiful.

620. If you get sunburned on vacation, sleep under a wet sheet or towel.

621. **BUY LOW SELL HIGH**: don't get that confused.

622. Allow one week or less to be disappointed, then re-group.

623. Appreciate Country and Western, "Hillbilly" music. They are America's folksongs.

624. Learn to take a power-nap.

625. Make your bed when you first get-up.

626. There is no substitute for fresh air.

627. Cut others some slack, every day.

628. Never awaken anybody with a list of things you want them to do.

629. Surprise them with breakfast in bed, instead. It's so easy.

630. Make popcorn on Sunday evenings.

631. Learn to cut hair.

632. Learn to give a good massage.

633. Sit in a hottub any chance you get.

634. If someone doesn't hear you, repeat your statement, pleasantly.

635. Tell someone when they hurt your feelings.

636. Know your limits in all things.

637. ***REMEMBER ALL THINGS END, EVEN BAD THINGS.***

638. Poverty is hereditary.

639. "If I have a lot to do, I take a nap first, to get that job out of the way." (Great Grandma Fishbach)

640. Contrary to popular opinion, turning up well-rested for a college final is no substitute for having studied.

641. Neurotics rarely become psychotic.

642. The genius of Woody Allen was to make us like New York and our own neurosis, through his. Can he succeed now that New York is more complicated and, apparently, so is he?

643. Betrayal is about mis-calculating another person's values.

644. Limit the number of activities you embrace where there is no substitute for victory.

645. Low self-esteem is a job only you can fix.

646. Keep your opinion of yourself a secret.

647. Simplify.

648. Americans have never understood the studied "British slam."

649. "Oh yeah?" is not a good comeback.

650. Neither is "shut-up and sit down!"

651. Desperate times make some leaders cynical and others inspiring.

652. Leadership is about putting people into jobs you know they'll do well.

653. "Coffee doesn't keep me awake, but it helps." (Grandpa Woods)

654. Never shorten someone's name without their permission.

655. It's too bad that we cannot easily see what we look like when we roll our eyes back in our heads.

656. Tears of joy have less to do with joy and more to do with the cessation of despair.

657. Call your brother or sister, just to talk.

658. Share with a child the miracle of watching a butterfly emerge from a caterpillar. Order a **LIVE BUTTERFLY CULTURE** from Insect Lore Products, P.O. Box 1535, Shafter, CA 93263 (1-800-LIVE BUG.)

659. Yet another division among people is those who like Mr. Rogers, and those who prefer Sesame Street.

660. Time wounds all heels.

661. Never confuse "legal," with "moral" or "right."

662. Never forget the stress of being in school.

663. Never forget the joys of being in school.

664. More than three quarters of what we learn is forgotten. (At least I think that's what I was told; or did I read that somewhere?)

665. Own a copy of Rick Nelson singing *"Garden Party."*

666. Watch Itzhak Perlman play the violin.

667. Happiness is a habit.

668. Happiness is a choice.

669. Appreciate handmade things.

670. Never lose your sense of wonder.

671. Research your family tree.

672. Know your family's health profile.

673. Never tell your mother "there's nothing to do," unless you are prepared to work.

674. If you default on a student loan, you must make restitution before you will be considered for a government-backed mortgage. Believe it.

675. To pay two extra mortgage payments a year is to bring down a thirty-year mortgage to a sixteen-year mortgage.

676. Don't compete with your children for their childhood.

677. ***YOU CAN NEVER BEAT YOUR FATHER: AT FIRST IT IS TOO HARD AND THEN IT IS TOO EASY.***

678. When your skill declines, your disposition needs to improve at the same rate.

679. Nothing looks worse than a young girl wearing clothes too sophisticated unless it's a matron wearing clothes too youthful.

680. Walk in the snow.

681. Feed the birds all year long.

682. Beware of humility with a hook. ("What, this ol' thing?")

683. Religion is supposed to make you loving and tolerant. If it isn't; it isn't working or you aren't.

684. Visit Monticello.

685. Read about Eleanor Roosevelt's life.

686. Have an aloe plant to treat burns and allergies.

687. Make certain that your child knows that "above the fruited plains," does not suggest a jet, decorated with bananas and grapes.

688. Internalize the words in the song "God Bless the Child."

689. An ice cube helps in the removal of chewing gum.

690. Petroleum jelly removes tar, pitch.

691. EVERY CHILD NEEDS A MOTHER AND A FATHER.

692. Every child needs someone soft and easily pleased. Every child needs someone firm, and harder to please. These roles are asexual.

1001 THINGS...   *Judy Woods-Knight*

693.   Unless you are a woman, never wear a hat indoors.

694.   When someone prefaces a remark with "I really hate to tell you this," they usually can't wait to tell you whatever they have to say.

695.   For an accurate insight into yourself and others, investigate the ***MYERS-BRIGGS TYPE INDICATOR.***

696.   *Please Understand Me* by Keirsey and Bates is an excellent book on the subject.

697.   If you believe "an action passed is an action completed," you had better be an adroit judge of co-workers competence.

698.   ***CRUTCHES ARE NOT INTRINSICALLY BAD.***

699.   Don't feel sorry for someone using a crutch or riding in a wheelchair; they've probably made a lot of progress.

700. If you have a cold, tell someone before being with them.

701. Most germs are transmitted through your hands. Wash them often.

702. Have "Ethnic Nights." Research exotic menus in the library and check out a record from the country you've chosen.

703. You can borrow not only records but cassettes, tapes and videos from your public library.

704. Store your woolen clothes in moth balls every summer.

705. Roast a turkey often; it's inexpensive and goes a long way.

706. Save your spice packets from Top Ramen to flavor homemade soups.

707. Never buy lawn furniture you have to move indoors when it rains.

708. See every movie Henry Fonda and Jimmy Stewart ever made. Except their westerns.

709. Put rubber bands around your playing cards.

710. ***BE A GOOD SPORT NO MATTER WHAT, WHERE, WHEN, WHY, HOW OR HOW OFTEN.***

711. How terrible to hate losing more than you enjoy winning.

712. ***IF YOU FEEL YOU NEED TO EXAGGERATE: UNDERESTIMATE.***

713. Every day is different.

714. Savor joy.

715. Save old perfume and after-shave bottles to capture a moment.

716. You can't claim to be "big-boned," if you're not. Your wrists and feet will give you away.

717. Clean your refrigerator every two weeks and put in an open box of baking soda.

718. Never give a child, or an older person, more than two instructions at a time.

719. Blend your own baby foods, especially fruits and vegetables.

720. Hippocrates said that all illness is emotionally induced.

721. Your heart does not stop when you sneeze.

722. There should be no conflict between Eastern and Western medicine, only a healthy blend.

723. Your heart is approximately the size of your fist. It is located roughly in the middle of your chest.

724. Take control of your life; don't live a "knee-jerk" existence.

725. **SUGAR IS BAD FOR YOU**; use substitutes whenever you can.

726. Even "natural sugar," is high in calories.

727. Never own a car without an air-conditioner unless you are a permanent resident of Nome, Alaska.

728. Never claim a state, strictly for a tax break.

729. *SUPPORT PRIVATE TV.*

730. Watch the Civil War series by Ken Burns, twice, at least.

731. Watch every thing the fabulous sisters, Olivia de Havilland and Joan Fontaine ever made.

732. Learn to make good gravy.

733. If you know someone who is about to have serious surgery, ask if you might be a blood donor.

734. Never ask someone to watch your dog for more than a week, unless it is the direst of emergencies.

735. *YOUR FACE WILL MIRROR YOUR ATTITUDE; MAKE IT PLEASANT.*

736. Don't save your best for the office. Bring some of it home.

737. A good driving record saves you a lot of money on your insurance.

738. So does a good scholastic record.

739. Save rainwater in containers to rinse your hair and hand wash items.

740. Use shampoo to hand wash delicate items.

741. To "sleep like a baby," could mean crying every two hours.

742. *NEVER SEND A POSTCARD TO PEOPLE WHILE YOU'RE ON VACATION UNLESS YOU'VE COMMUNICATED WITH THEM, RECENTLY.*

743. Never plan to permanently park a car, boat, trailer or RV in your cul-de-sac or front of your neighbor's house unless 1) you read the covenants 2) you've asked them 3) you have no other choice.

744. *NEVER RENT OR BUY A HOME WITH MORE YARDWORK THAN YOU CARE TO DO.*

745. Use products such as "Miracle Grow," liberally.

746. Keep your address book up-to-date.

747. When you move, take your phone book. You will be surprised how many times you need that reference.

748. Be careful about asking a person what they do for a living.

749. Offer to be a reference for people you think might need one.

750. Everyone you meet has a fascinating story.

751. Never leave your laundry unattended in an laundromat.

752. Volunteer in a hospital.

753. See the ocean as often as possible.

754. Depression: A time to doubt your worth.

755. If you worry about having Alzheimer's disease, you don't.

756. Many people develop Alzheimer's disease, but many more have "Sometimer's disease."

757. Don't complicate your doctor visit with frantic, random questions; bring a list of vital questions you need answered.

758. Always carry with you pictures or mementos which make you happy.

759. *NEVER THRUST YOURSELF UPON ANYONE*.

760. Accept the challenge to understand your insurance policies.

761. Write a prompt thank you note for a meal, a gift given, an over-night visit or a thoughtful gesture.

Judy Woods-Knight *1001 THINGS...*

762. ***CELEBRATE THE SEASONS.***

763. In winter make Gluh Wein, spicy tea.

764. In the fall, "winter" your outdoor flower baskets by placing them where it's warm; watering them occasionally.

765. In early spring cut branches and put them in water to force an early bloom.

766. When it's summer, grow tomatoes and make your own salsa.

767. At the end of a job-well done, reward yourself; you know what you'd like and you know what you've accomplished.

768. If you work in an office without a window, hang travel posters.

769. Decorate blank walls at home the same way. You can get posters free from some travel agencies.

770. Use push tacks rather than nails whenever possible.

771. No one should celebrate Thanksgiving Day without including someone who might not have a very good day otherwise.

772. Everyone should investigate the life of Christopher Columbus and reach their own conclusions.

773. ***HAVE A CURIOUS MIND: DON'T TAKE ANYTHING YOU READ, HEAR, THINK, FEEL, OR SEE, FOR GRANTED.***

774. Never suppose your religion to be the only means of salvation.

775. If someone you know has a Master's degree, ask to read their thesis. Even if it's ancient or obscure, find something positive to say about it. (Wow! That was really informative!)

776. If you like to write poetry, know that we currently have a society dead to poets.

777. "I'm a poet and I didn't even think I was." (Jeffrey C. Knight)

1001 THINGS...   *Judy Woods-Knight*

778. Don't expect to achieve what your parents have, too soon.

779. Everybody's got to pay their dues.

780. ***NOTHING IS QUITE AS EASY AS IT SEEMS.***

781. That which comes too easily is not always lasting.

782. If your spouse is not your best friend, your life will always be difficult.

783. If your spouse is not your best friend, don't substitute your child into that role.

784. With very few exceptions, your spouse wants to be your friend; work on that reality.

785. Most of us enjoy wallowing in feelings of groundless despair.

786. We are not so receptive to feelings of groundless joy.

787. In the Christian theology, the Holy Spirit is a neglected source of strength and wisdom.

788. Rightfully, it takes a great deal of preparation and study to obtain a driver's license.

789. Incredibly, it takes virtually no effort to obtain a marriage license.

790. Pre-nuptial agreements are often unromantic necessities.

791. The women's liberation movement has made it reasonable for women to pay alimony.

792. *WOMEN ARE THE LONGEST LIVED MAMMALS ON THE FACE OF THE EARTH*.

793. Although we have a reputation for being "fragile," women are tough, flexible, receptive and adaptable to all kinds of change.

794. Who wants to be female and alone at ninety-three?

795. *MEN SHOULD APPRECIATE THE SECRETS WOMEN KNOW.*

796. *WOMEN SHOULD APPRECIATE THE SECRETS MEN KNOW.*

797. *UNISEX IS BORING.*

798. Different capabilities do not degrade you.

799. Don't take on a job you're going to complain about later.

800. Don't display books you have not read.

801. Bill Bryson has written a hilarious book on travel entitled *Neither Here Nor There*, published by William Morrow & Company.

802. Mr. Bryson advises us to cross busy streets in foreign countries "as though we had bull's eyes painted on our butts."

803. Mr. Bryson was being conservative.

804. Know that toilet paper in foreign countries has all the charm of packing material.

805. When ordering anything in Germany, know that your thumb counts as "one." To disregard this is to receive three beers, every time.

806. If you are relying on English as you tour foreign lands, speak slowly not loudly.

807. Learn to eat Chinese food with chopsticks. It tastes even better that way.

808. Watch an Oriental eat; they bring their bowls under their chins; they spear, scoop and slop, just like you will.

809. Orientals use beaded curtains over open doors to cut down on flies.

810. Mexicans hang plastic sacks of water over their open doors for the same purpose.

811. Visit grocery stores in foreign countries. It's interesting and can save you a lot of money and grief over choosing souvenir items.

812. Local cookbooks make good souvenirs on trips taken, anywhere.

813. Use the small refrigerator, in most hotels, to store things you can't do without.

814. If you only have wire hangers, put newspaper over them to hang your trousers.

815. To freshen a wrinkled garment, put it in the bathroom while you take a shower, or on the balcony.

816. Resist the temptation to display decals of your travels on your car.

817. *AMERICA IS THE MOST ADMIRED AND IMITATED COUNTRY IN THE WORLD.*

818. When in New York, don't ask a cab driver where to eat unless you want to dine at his cousin's establishment.

819. When you are in a foreign country ask the concierge to write down the address of both your hotel and where you want to go before ordering a cab.

820. Many a trip is happier in the reliving.

821. Everyone should learn to light a good fireplace fire.

822. Everyone should learn to light a campfire.

823. All you need for a camping trip is a blanket, a frying pan, matches, a safety pin and string. (John B. Woods, Jr. Forester)

824. After you have bathed your dog, use your hair conditioner on him/her.

825. There are some animals which shouldn't be bathed; gerbils, birds, hamsters are but a few.

826. Always offer someone who looks worse off than you, your seat on a bus.

827. A man always walks on the traffic side of a sidewalk.

828. Own a Sears' catalogue. It's a good reference.

829. Begin your Christmas shopping during the after-Christmas sales.

830. Never charge anything you can put on lay-away.

831. Never send a Christmas card without a handwritten greeting.

832. Read Winston Churchill's series The Second World War.

833. Nobody hates war more than a soldier; except a soldier's wife.

834. Never take money from the military if you have any reservations about serving in a crisis.

835. Don't marry a soldier if you don't like the life.

836. Never marry anyone whose career doesn't work with yours.

837. Decide before you are married if and when you want children.

838. Try to imagine holidays and "old age" if you don't have them.

839. It's cheaper to fund Democracy than to defend it.

840. Have faith; put your name and number in the telephone book.

1001 THINGS... *Judy Woods-Knight*

841. ***YOU WILL PROBABLY LOVE MANY PEOPLE IN YOUR LIFETIME.***

842. These attractions will enhance your life only if they don't interfere with it.

843. Appreciate the laugh of Richard Dreyfuss.

844. Appreciate Whoopi Goldberg for a host of reasons.

845. To understand another culture, ethnic group, listen to their comics. They you tell the truth and make you like it.

846. The royal scandals have a decidedly American flavor in that they are totally out-of-hand, exquisitely painful, private, embarrassing, persistent, probably insolvable and have ramifications which could undermine a culture.

847. Princess Diana is a lovely, wounded bird.

848. Prince Charles has been trained to shoot birds, not heal them.

849. Don't take sides in issues that are none of your business.

850. *OPINIONS ARE LIKE RECTUMS: EVERYBODY HAS ONE.*

851. *SOMETIMES TO WIN IS TO LOSE; THE PROCESS IS CALLED BEING DEAD RIGHT.*

852. In Real Estate, the fussiest buyer is often the one who has the least money.

853. If you sell your house too quickly, you will suppose your price was too low.

854. If you think America is in chaos, visit another country.

855. The American phone system is second to none. So is CNN.

856. **AN EXPERT**: One who passes out with pragmatic fortitude, infinite pages of incomprehensible formulae, calibrated with micrometric precision from vague assumptions which are based on debatable figures taken from inconclusive experiments carried out with instruments of questionable accuracy by deceased or anonymous technicians of doubtful reliability and refutable credentials.

857. **A CONSULTANT**: Someone with a briefcase, at least two hours from home.

858. **IN COMMERCE**: A slowing up of the slow down is worse than an upturn in the slow down. It's better, though, than a speed up of the slow down or a deepening of the down turn. Got that?

859. The secret to success in the business world is to have the right excuse.

860. That's how we've always done it.

861. I didn't know there was a rush.

862. That's not my area.

863. No one told me.

864. I was waiting for further instructions.

865. I didn't know this project was "special."

866. I did it "on accident."

867. I told you I couldn't do it.

868. I was too busy.

869. I lost it.

870. The computer was down.

871. I've been sick.

872. ***IF YOU FIND SOMETHING THAT MAKES YOUR LIFE EASIER, KNOW THAT SOMEWHERE, SOMEONE IS PLOTTING TO MAKE THAT PRODUCT UNAVAILABLE.***

873. Learn how to present new ideas as progress not treason.

874. ***INDECISION LOOKS A LOT LIKE FLEXIBILITY.***

875. There is nothing that comes close to a genuine lack of preparation.

876. Happiness is a lot more than a remission of pain.

877. Deja vu has happened before and nostalgia isn't what it used to be.

878. Different opinions made horse racing.

879. It's hard to write interesting memoirs if you haven't taken any chances.

880. Nobody sets out to write a bad book, or make a bad movie.

881. Spot your heavy work with heavy relaxation.

882. Never call an office for a big decision on Friday.

883. Use the phrase "what's your opinion?" often.

884. The most dispensable letter in the alphabet is the capital "i."

885. Never say "this'll be easy to fix."

886. Machiavelli, in l513 wrote: "There is nothing more difficult to plan, more doubtful of success, or more dangerous to manage than the creation of a new system for the initiator has the enmity of all who would profit by the preservation of the old system and merely lukewarm defenders in those who would gain by the new one."

887. **COORDINATOR**: A person from HQ sent to make everyone feel nervous and inadequate.

888. **WE'RE MAKING A SURVEY**: We need more time to think up an excuse.

889. **UNDER CONSIDERATION**: We don't remember anything about it.

890. **UNDER ACTIVE CONSIDERATION**: We don't remember anything about it and can prove it.

891. **WE WILL INVESTIGATE**: Only if we're certain of the outcome.

892. **RELIABLE SOURCE**: Almost anyone.

893. **UNIMPEACHABLE SOURCE**: Someone whose name we remember.

894. **SEE ME LATER ON THIS**: I will bully you, privately.

895. **WILL ADVISE YOU IN DUE COURSE**: Don't call us....

896. **NEVER BRING A PROBLEM TO YOUR BOSS WITHOUT AT LEAST TWO POSSIBLE SOLUTIONS.**

897. **INCOMPLETE VOCABULARY FOR GOVERNMENT EMPLOYEES:**

898. **IT'S IN PROGRESS:** You are aware of backwards progress?

899. **WE WILL LOOK INTO IT:** We will? Where? How?

900. **A PROBLEM:** Anything that cannot be handled with a memo or a phone call.

901. **WE WILL EXPEDITE**: Everything is relative.

902. **WE WILL WORK IT THROUGH CHANNELS**: Where we expect it to get hopelessly lost.

903. **TECHNICAL ADVISOR**: Someone who can't make it in a real job.

904. **TO ACTIVATE:** To make busy work look good.

905. **TO IMPLEMENT**: To shove an ill-conceived plan on people who don't want it, don't understand it and expect them to make it work.

906. **UNDER CONSIDERATION**: The main consideration is finding the project so we can properly reject it.

907. **UNDER ACTIVE CONSIDERATION**: Somebody remembers rejecting the plan but they can't remember notifying anyone about it.

908. **A MEETING**: A time to come together to find reasons why the new project won't work.

909. **A CONFERENCE**: A scenario for fine tuning the blame.

910. **TO NEGOTIATE**: A time to find a solution everybody hates.

911. **REORIENTATION**: Blame assessment with old friends.

912. **CLARIFICATION:** An opportunity to fill in some data supporting the conclusions we made long ago.

913. **WE ARE MAKING A SURVEY:** We have to find a few more people who agree with us on this matter.

914. **NOTE AND INITIAL**: Let's spread the blame.

915. **LET'S GET TOGETHER ON THIS**: Or you'll miss Christmas, Easter....

916. **SEE ME**: You are in deep gumbo.

917. **GIVE US THE BENEFIT OF YOUR THINKING**: As long as it does not differ from what we hope has been clearly alluded to as our thinking.

918. **WE WILL ADVISE YOU IN DUE COURSE**: We're hoping you'll forget all about it, just as we plan to do.

919. **LET ME GIVE YOU THE BIG PICTURE**: *My* big picture.

920. **APPROVED SUBJECT TO APPROVAL**: We are starting over.

921. **IT'S POLICY**: Thank God; we don't have to think.

922. **KEEP A LOW PROFILE**: In the best tradition of most snakes.

923. *NEVER PROMISE MORE THAN YOU CAN DO; NEVER DO MORE THAN YOU PROMISE.*

924. *LEARN TO REPEAT THINGS, EXACTLY; EXACTLY!*

925. *ALWAYS BE OVER PREPARED AT A MEETING BUT DON'T FEEL COMPELLED TO PROVE THAT YOU ARE.*

926. There is a big difference between knowing and understanding.

927. There is a big difference between presenting and motivating.

928. ***NEVER WORK FOR, CONFIDE IN, TRUST, GIVE WATER OR SUSTENANCE TO A PERSON WHO REFERS TO A WOMAN AS A "NON-MALE."***

929. To kill a slug, put beer in a pie tin; they die happy.

930. Don't expect praise for a job, well done.

931. Do expect criticism for a job, mis-handled.

932. Don't invite people to visit, flippantly. ("Ya'll come?")

933. Never give a guest your bed. You will both be uncomfortable.

934. Never talk about your finances; if you're broke you'll make people nervous, if you're rich, you'll make them envious. If you're doing fine, what's the point?

935. When someone informs you that they are "at death's door," resist the temptation to tell them that "you hope they'll pull through."

936. Don't get a tattoo. If you do, never tell your mother. Ever.

937. Never take anyone wearing an ankle bracelet seriously.

938. "Too assume is to make an ass of 'u' and 'me.'"
(Tony Randall from TV's Odd Couple.)

939. **GOLF**: an expensive walk around a beautiful area where the positioning of a small white ball can make you hate both yourself and your surroundings.

940. **SKIING**: A prohibitively expensive interlude in a beautiful area which you will not notice because you are trying to save your life.

941. Don't involve yourself in any sport with rescue missions.

942. In tropical climates, such as Mexico and Thailand, they eat hot, spicy food.

943. In the Scandinavian countries, where it's cold and dark, they eat little open-faced sandwiches decorated with bits of dead fish.

944. The church bell you found so charming during the day may lose it's allure during the night.

945. The reason your grandmother told you to say out of drafts was that your body is forced to use energy it needs to fight germs to keep an even temperature. The process is called **HOMEOSTASIS**.

946. There is something wrong when an insurance company is allowed to cancel its sickest clients.

947. The time to buy insurance is when you are young and healthy; no matter how broke you are.

948. A wise person knows when they are not addressing the man, but his weariness, his frustration, his sadness, his disease.

949. Eddy Murphy's "**RAW**" wasn't raw, it was half-baked.

950. **A PROPHET IS NOT A PROPHET IN HIS OWN LAND** due in part to their intensity which makes them card carrying pains.

951. "My mind has a mind of its own." (Jean C. Woods)

952. **BUNGEE JUMPING**: A perfect sport for those who have fun and fear confused.

953. **PMS IS BOTH REAL AND TERRIBLE.**

954. Erma Bombeck suggested sending a troop of women PMS sufferers to fight the Saudi's but the UN wouldn't hear of it!

955. Charlie Brown is boring.

956. For better or for worse, society put Dagwood's Blondie to work.

957. When I was ten, I was told that blue and green clashed. When I was twenty, I was informed that denying sex to my husband was a mortal sin. When I was thirty, I was told I was over the hill "obstetrically." When I was forty I was told staying at home and raising a family was not satisfying. When I was fifty I was told that my life was on the downhill slope. What are you hearing now that simply isn't true?

958. **WHAT DO WOMEN WANT?** A woman wants to be incredibly beautiful at every stage of her life. She wants a stomach that is concave and an exorbitantly wealthy husband whom she has helped,

every step of the way. She wants to be adored by him and her two point five children who excel in virtually everything, yet make no demands on her time. She wants her husband's support in all of her endeavors. Yet, she needs for him to encourage her independence and capability all the while providing her with safe but incredibly euphoric sex. She wants a pedigreed pooch who requires no grooming and awakens only to pee-pee and perform an amazing trick or three. She wants a fascinating circle of friends who consider her mere attendance at their function a honor of the highest sort. She wants to travel extensively and to be on a first name basis with all the swells of the world. She wishes to be an **ATHLETIC HEALTH GODDESS**, endowed with unobtrusive muscles that require no tiresome maintenance. She wishes that the Pope would call her for an audience, and that scheduling it would create a real problem; for someone else. She wants meaningful, creative work in a setting where her unique talents and contributions are appreciated to the extent that she is allowed to write her own schedule. She'd like to make Jackie Onassis look "frumpy," Mother Theresa "selfish" and William F. Buckley "sophomoric."

959. **WHAT DO MEN WANT?** Men want vast amounts of success, respect, sports, steak, sex, beer, and space.

960. Almost everyone has a nightmare in which they are hurrying to a final exam in a class they have not attended.

961. It is our observation that Americans line up better and drive more cautiously than any other culture.

962. Feel sad when people burn the flag.

963. Symbols are important; that's why they do it.

964. Be on your toes when a member of your family informs you that "a car in front of me was rear-ended."

965. No matter how creative you are, it's hard to explain to your insurance company that you backed into your own vehicle.

1001 THINGS... *Judy Woods-Knight*

966. Beware of a woman buying an accent piece. It may be the "advance man" for a redecorating scheme or a whole new wardrobe.

967. Surprise your wife on some distant anniversary with the largest diamond you can almost afford. With it, enclose a card, pledging your love and devotion for the rest of your life. (Trust us on this one.)

968. Tuna Surprise was so named by the cook who was surprised that anyone ate it.

969. Beware of the child who wants you to type their paper at the last minute.

970. Your worse suspicions will be realized when they ask you to "tighten it up some."

971. The definition of "tightening up a term paper;" to correct the spelling, grammar, punctuation, content, organization, references, footnotes and bibliography. It may also mean the addition of verbs.

972. If someone "eats like a bird," remember the pelican.

973. Never believe it when someone declares that they were just certain they told you.

974. When somebody says "as you already know...." they either don't remember themselves or simply can't bear to rehash it.

975. **WOMAN TO WOMAN**: Never refer to another woman as "my best friend."

976. If you own a private business or enterprise, even your best friends will want items or services at cost.

977. On Valentine's Day, give your spouse a list of all the things you like about them.

978. Tenderness in a couple long married speaks well of each partner.

1001 THINGS...   *Judy Woods-Knight*

979. Never say "my wife made me everything I am today," if you are broke, bald, and miserable.

980. Mutually gratifying sex happens when the partners love each other and themselves.

981. Never step on anybody's dream, no matter how preposterous it is.

982. You can fake a lot of things but not a quick wit.

983. ***NOBODY LOVES SUMMER MORE THAN A TEACHER.***

984. You may not be as good as you once were, but you can be as good, once, as you ever were.

985. Being a perfectionist is a self-serving, dangerous trait.

986. Be satisfied with a lot less than perfection from your children if you want them to keep on trying.

987. Learn to do small things well.

988. Be happy with the talents you have.

989. ***NEVER LAUGH AT SOMEONE WHO HAS FALLEN AND CAN'T GET UP.***

990. ***THE SECRET TO A HAPPY LIFE IS HOPE.***

991. To consider yourself as the center of the universe is to spin like a top.

992. Life is so short and death is so long.

993. It's a lot easier to live and to die if you believe in an after-life.

994. Highly intelligent people seem to have a difficult time living a happy life.

995. Nothing exceeds like excess.

996. ***PRO-CHOICE SHOULD NOT BEGIN IN AN ABORTION CLINIC.***

997. Most of life's truth's have to be learned first hand.

998. When confidence fades, rely on courage.

999. You may have to plant the roses you want to smell someday.

1000. ***TOO MUCH IS TOO MUCH, TOO LITTLE IS TOO LITTLE, ENOUGH IS ENOUGH.***

1001. Happiness is what happens after we have kissed all of life's ugly little frogs.

—OKAY TO COPY COUPON—

More Quality Books from R & E Publishers

TAKING CHARGE: A Parent and Teacher Guide to Loving Discipline by Jo Anne Nordling. At last, here is a book that shows both parents and teachers everything they need to know to discipline children effectively and fairly.

This easy-to-understand action guide will show you how to handle the most critical disciplinary issues in teaching and raising children.

$11.95	LC 91-50985	ISBN 0-88247-906-7
Trade Paper	6x9	Order #906-7

THE GOAL BOOK: Your Simple Power Guide to Reach any Goal & Get What You Want by James Hall. Would you like to be able to turn your dreams into realities? You can if you have concrete goals. This book is based upon a unique goal achievement technique developed by a high school teacher and career counselor in California's Silicon Valley. "Action Conditioning Technology" (ACT) will help you convert your dreams and wishful fantasies into obtainable goals. With this new achievement technology, you will be able to decide exactly what you want, what steps you need to take and when you will reach your objective.

$6.95	LC 91-50675	ISBN 0-88247-892-3
Trade paper	6 x 9	Order #892-3

FOR TEACHERS ONLY: Personal and Confidential by William Sorrells. Teachers are the most poorly treated, and poorly paid professionals in this country. *For Teachers Only: Personal and Confidential—The Secret Files of a Veteran Teacher* exposes the shocking treatment that leads to low self-esteem and job burnout among this nation's educators. Author William Sorrells has issued an emancipation proclamation for teachers that will help them to reclaim their power and restore the vision that originally lead them to become teachers. His book offers specific actions that every teacher must take to increase their own self-worth. Only in this way, Sorrells tells us, can we reverse the trends that are undermining the very fabric of our educational system.

$9.95	ISBN 0-88247-889-3	LC 91-52960
Trade paper	Order #889-3	6 x 9

THE SOLUTION STRATEGY: Your Handbook for Solving Life's Problems by Phil McWilliams. If you didn't have any problems, what would you do? You'd probably be reading *The Solution Strategy* by Phil McWilliams. He has written the one book you need to solve *any* problem. Now you can stop relying on luck or guesswork to handle difficult situations. With this step-by-step technique you'll be able to determine where your problems come from, how to identify them and then—eliminate them. You'll learn how to overcome problems through the integration of emotions and intellect. Once you learn these techniques, you'll be able to accomplish any goal. *The Solution Strategy* is not Pop Psychology or Religion. It is a new kind of self-help book that really works!

$9.95   LC 91-61309   ISBN 0-88247-875-3

Trade paper   6x9   Order #875-3

1001 THINGS WE WOULD HAVE TOLD OUR KIDS HAD THEY EVER LISTENED

JUDY WOODS KNIGHT

Mark Twain said that when he was a boy, he was convinced that his father was stupid. But by the time he became a man, he was amazed at how much his father had learned. Take our advice and read this handy little user's guide to life. Buy one for your children and let them see how smart you really are.

___ $6.95   Soft Cover   ISBN 0-88247-989-10   Order #989-10

YOUR ORDER				Please rush me the following books. I want to save by ordering three books and receive FREE shipping charges. Orders under 3 books please include $2.50 shipping. CA residents add 8.25% tax.
ORDER #	QTY	UNIT PRICE	TOTAL PRICE	

SHIP TO:

(Please Print) Name: _____

Organization: _____

Address: _____

City/State/Zip: _____

PAYMENT METHOD

Enclosed check or money order

MasterCard   Card Expires _____ Signature _____

Visa

R & E Publishers • P.O. Box 2008 • Saratoga, CA 95070 (408) 866-6303

—OKAY TO COPY COUPON—

More Quality Books from R & E Publishers

TAKING CHARGE: A Parent and Teacher Guide to Loving Discipline by Jo Anne Nordling. At last, here is a book that shows both parents and teachers everything they need to know to discipline children effectively and fairly.

This easy-to-understand action guide will show you how to handle the most critical disciplinary issues in teaching and raising children.

$11.95	LC 91-50985	ISBN 0-88247-906-7
Trade Paper	6x9	Order #906-7

THE GOAL BOOK: Your Simple Power Guide to Reach any Goal & Get What You Want by James Hall. Would you like to be able to turn your dreams into realities? You can if you have concrete goals. This book is based upon a unique goal achievement technique developed by a high school teacher and career counselor in California's Silicon Valley. "Action Conditioning Technology" (ACT) will help you convert your dreams and wishful fantasies into obtainable goals. With this new achievement technology, you will be able to decide exactly what you want, what steps you need to take and when you will reach your objective.

$6.95	LC 91-50675	ISBN 0-88247-892-3
Trade paper	6 x 9	Order #892-3

FOR TEACHERS ONLY: Personal and Confidential by William Sorrells. Teachers are the most poorly treated, and poorly paid professionals in this country. *For Teachers Only: Personal and Confidential—The Secret Files of a Veteran Teacher* exposes the shocking treatment that leads to low self-esteem and job burnout among this nation's educators. Author William Sorrells has issued an emancipation proclamation for teachers that will help them to reclaim their power and restore the vision that originally lead them to become teachers. His book offers specific actions that every teacher must take to increase their own self-worth. Only in this way, Sorrells tells us, can we reverse the trends that are undermining the very fabric of our educational system.

$9.95		LC 91-52960
Trade paper	ISBN 0-88247-889-3	6 x 9
	Order #889-3	

THE SOLUTION STRATEGY: Your Handbook for Solving Life's Problems by Phil McWilliams. If you didn't have any problems, what would you do? You'd probably be reading *The Solution Strategy* by Phil McWilliams. He has written the one book you need to solve *any* problem. Now you can stop relying on luck or guesswork to handle difficult situations. With this step-by-step technique you'll be able to determine where your problems come from, how to identify them and then—eliminate them. You'll learn how to overcome problems through the integration of emotions and intellect. Once you learn these techniques, you'll be able to accomplish any goal. *The Solution Strategy* is not Pop Psychology or Religion. It is a new kind of self-help book that really works!

$9.95   LC 91-61309   ISBN 0-88247-875-3
Trade paper   6x9   Order #875-3

1001 THINGS WE WOULD HAVE TOLD OUR KIDS HAD THEY EVER LISTENED

JUDY WOODS KNIGHT

Mark Twain said that when he was a boy, he was convinced that his father was stupid. But by the time he became a man, he was amazed at how much his father had learned. Take our advice and read this hand little user's guide to life. Buy one for your children and let them see how smart you really are.

$6.95   Soft Cover   ISBN 0-88247-989-10   Order #989-10

YOUR ORDER

ORDER #	QTY	UNIT PRICE	TOTAL PRICE

Please rush me the following books. I want to save by ordering three books and receive FREE shipping charges. Orders under 3 books please include $2.50 shipping. CA residents add 8.25% tax.

SHIP TO:

(Please Print) Name: _____
Organization: _____
Address: _____
City/State/Zip: _____

PAYMENT METHOD

Enclosed check or money order
MasterCard   Card Expires _____ Signature _____
Visa

R & E Publishers • P.O. Box 2008 • Saratoga, CA 95070 (408) 866-6303